# Learn To
# With Sp
# And Success!

Whether you are an executive, a secretary, a lawyer, a salesperson, a teacher—or anything in between—you must be able to think before you speak, if you want to make the most of your potential. HOW TO THINK ON YOUR FEET gives you the insights, tools, and techniques you need to:

**BUILD GOOD RELATIONSHIPS**

Be a welcome conversationalist by giving responses that encourage responses.

**BE A WINNER**

Learn the five basic steps for success in responding to all questions, from when to listen to when to say more.

**HEDGE, BUT STILL BE IN CONTROL**

Here's the secret of saying "it's none of your business" in socially acceptable, conversationally appropriate terms.

**BE DIRECT**

Polish your delivery so that you can tackle tough questions with forthright answers.

**BE CANDID—AND CREDIBLE!**

You can say "I don't know, but..." and still be convincing.

This remarkable book will help you sharpen your communication skills—and transform your life. Over 10,000 readers agree that its theories and tactics have made them more confident, more articulate...and successful.

# HOW TO THINK
## ON YOUR FEET

(original title: *Thinking on Your Feet*)

## Marian K. Woodall

**WARNER BOOKS**

A Time Warner Company

WARNER BOOKS EDITION

Copyright © 1990, 1993 by Marian K. Woodall
All rights reserved.

This Warner Books Edition is published by arrangement with the author.

Cover design by Diane Luger
Cover illustration by Tom Stimpson

Warner Books, Inc.
1271 Avenue of the Americas
New York, NY 10020

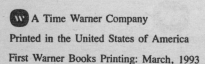 A Time Warner Company

Printed in the United States of America

First Warner Books Printing: March, 1993

10 9 8 7 6 5 4 3 2 1

# ACKNOWLEDGMENTS

My special thanks to:

The thousands of college students whose challenging questions during our classes these last twenty-four years spurred my creative efforts to develop these response techniques.

The hundreds of business professionals who have heard me present this material as "Impromptu Responses," as "Responding to Questions," as a part of "One-to-One Communication Skills," and as "Thinking on Your Feet"—because their continued requests for "a book" or "some tapes" gave me the initial incentive for this step.

Dr. Gretchen Vik of San Diego State University, Linda Marshall of Schwabe, Williamson and Wyatt, and a fellow writer, my brother Bill Woodall, who each added thoughtful comments in their critique of the manuscript.

My parents, for an upbringing which encouraged creativity and initiative.

My husband, Kent Franklin, who continues to provide support and encouragement.

# Contents

# Preface

Thinking on your feet means considering what you want to communicate, so that when you begin to speak, you are truly ready. Learning to think on your feet requires that you learn to buy time to think beforehand. This book takes you through that entire process, from thought to answer, from glimmer of idea to comment. It provides you with the key to success—the tools for buying time to think. It also gives you insights, a little theory, and a great variety of examples to examine.

This book began in the 1970s as a lecture called "Impromptu Responses." Webster defines *impromptu* as "without preparation; offhand." And that phrase clearly defines the problem people have in two communicating situations: when they are asked to speak unexpectedly and when they are asked a question. People who speak without sufficient forethought sound unprepared; their comments or answers sound not thought out. Sounding unprepared is a problem simply because you should be able to talk comfortably about whatever topic you wish. Sounding unprepared means that you lose your poise, followed closely by a loss of confidence—both yours and your listeners'. What happens next? You lose your credibility. The premise of this book is that you could answer or comment well if you thought briefly before you spoke.

My early presentations on Impromptu Responses evolved, as such material does, through audience participation and reactions. Since the major concern of my listeners was how to answer questions, this book deals primarily with strategies and tips for responding better to questions, especially difficult ones. To deal more successfully with questions it is important to observe the patterns of questions and what type of response each seeks (chapter 3). Understanding questions enables you to respond better—and you may even ask your own questions a bit more carefully.

Critical to the discussion of questions and answers is an understanding of how successful communication occurs. The most frequent communication that humans have—in business as well as in their personal and social lives—is in their conversations. For a conversation to be successful, more is needed than just questions and answers. Chapter 3 explains what else is needed.

Finally, there are those unexpected opportunities that you have to say a few words about something—though my reaction is that when you are involved in a project, no opportunity should be unexpected. The essential strategies for commenting are the same as those for responding to questions. Special considerations are discussed in chapter 13.

So, if your goal is to communicate successfully with others, you will want to master thinking on your feet. If you are concerned about responding positively in tense situations—rather than saying something you later would give anything to take back—plan to master the skill of thinking on your feet. If you want to appear poised and confident when put on the spot, learn to think on your feet.

*Master* is the key word in your approach to the following material. There you will find specific new techniques for answering questions and making impromptu comments. You will also be reminded of approaches you have used but may not always remember to use when you need them. If you wish to make the most of yourself, develop tools that you can use. Then practice, practice, practice. Your results will be the three goals suggested in chapter 1:

- effective communications
- improved human relations
- credibility and poise

Be poised, and be powerful!

—Marian K. Woodall

# CHAPTER 1

# What Does It Mean to Think on Your Feet and Why Is It Important?

To think on your feet is to say exactly what you want to say, whether you are standing or seated. To think on your feet is to say the appropriate thing at the right moment—during your conversation, not after you hang up the telephone or leave the room.

Thinking on your feet means having credibility when you respond or speak extemporaneously. Thinking on your feet also means sounding assertive when you wish not to be bested as a consumer. It means creating the best impression possible when you interview for a job. Thinking on your feet especially means responding to questions—all questions, both the routine and the challenging—equally well.

Thinking on your feet is not about "blowing smoke."

This important communication skill means being in control. It means appearing and sounding professional no

**5**

matter who asks you a question or what the question is. It means appearing and sounding professional no matter where you are and to what comment you are responding.

## Goals of Thinking on Your Feet

There are three significant goals to master in thinking on your feet:

- effective communications
- improved human relationships
- credibility and poise

Communicating with others on a one-to-one basis is a fact of life that many people take for granted. We shouldn't. Effective communication means a great deal more than just getting the right words out. Part of communication is the words, true. But more of it—much more of it—is the nonverbal message that is conveyed by the words.

Nonverbal communication is so important, in fact, that if you are receiving a mixed message—the words communicate one message, the nonverbal another—the nonverbal message will usually be the truer one. How does all this relate to thinking on your feet? It's basic: If you blurt out the first thing that comes to your mind, without thought or planning, you will often be faced with results you do not like. And if you say something that isn't true, your nonverbal message will contradict your words.

So, thinking on your feet also means being confident that all of what you communicate is appropriate—your verbal message will be consistent with your nonverbal message. Your communication will be effective, your human relations will be good, and your poise and credibility will be intact.

## An Easy Skill to Master

Saying the appropriate thing at the appropriate time is a skill that almost everyone can master. You can learn to think on your feet with the same unconscious ease with which you hit a great golf shot, bake a perfect pie crust, close a difficult sale, or interpret a balance sheet. With practice you will be able to think on your feet without even having to think about what tools are involved.

## How Do You Learn This Communication Skill?

As in learning any skill, there are two basic steps: first, learn the techniques; second, practice them. In this book you will first learn tips for general success and the specific techniques or tactics to use in various difficult communications situations. Next, you will be instructed to practice these techniques by yourself, with others in your family, and with your co-workers, until they become second nature. Use an audio tape or, better, a videotape to hear and see which areas you have mastered and those you need to improve. The key to success is practice, practice, practice.

## Why Is It Important to Think on Your Feet?

Thinking on your feet is important for many reasons that you already know: confidence, credibility, appearing and sounding professional, making an impressive appearance, looking and sounding unflappable, and being known as a person to rely on in a difficult situation.

*Confidence.* You must be confident to think on your feet successfully. Just the fact that you know you can do it makes you more confident in all other communications activities. Knowing you won't be embarrassed adds to that confident feeling. Realizing that others will not be able to put you down or leave you at a loss for words further enhances your confidence.

*Credibility.* To have credibility, your words and the surrounding nonverbal messages need to match.

*Appearing and sounding professional.* No one can know all the answers all the time. But don't your customers (or your students, or your subordinates, or your clients) think you should? How do you look (and feel) when you are asked a question to which you must hedge in response? When hedging it's even more important to remain in control, in order to maintain people's trust and respect—and their business! When people ask questions, often what they really want to know is, "Are you reliable?" or, "Are you in charge here?" or, "Do you know what you're talking about?" or, "Will my money [or stocks, or automobile, or clothes, or kids, or...] be safe with you?"

*Creating an impression.* The impression you leave with people is frequently much more important than the information you give them. Nonverbal gestures, verbal delivery (including speed, emphasis, and tone), and body posture send the impression that the customer or client receives and responds to. Thinking on your feet enables you to be certain that the impression they receive is positive. People think: *She's very professional; he knows what he's doing.*

*Appearing unflappable.* When you are the kind of person people cannot fluster, they will soon learn that and quit trying. If being asked direct, pointed questions no longer puts you on the spot, people will tend not to ask them. If being called upon unexpectedly does not throw you, you will be considered unflappable. An unflappable person is relied on and admired. Reactions tend to be, "Say, you can't catch him napping. He's on top of everything," and "I admire a person who handles things without getting all bent out of shape."

*Being known as reliable in difficult situations.* You are the kind of person who is given more responsibility, quicker promotions, and awarded those difficult or risky client contacts that pay such fine dividends when they are successfully handled. Your boss's reaction? "Jane's the person for the Folger Brothers; with her abilities to answer their picky little questions, she'll get that account for sure."

Learning to think on your feet will reward you in many more ways than you can imagine. Resolve to learn the tools and develop this skill—today.

# CHAPTER 2
# Do You Need to Think on Your Feet?

Probably.

You need to think on your feet if you are a doctor, lawyer, consultant, or an accountant. If you speak to the press—that means politicians, bureau chiefs, city council members, candidates for office—you need to think before you speak. If you are answerable to a board of directors or to stockholders, thinking on your feet is a requirement of your job. (Won't you be proud of yourself when you can smile warmly at that old goat who always tries to pin you down at the annual meeting? You can dispatch his whiny, negative question with a firm, positive response.)

You also need to speak well on your feet if you are a sales representative who calls on clients, a retail sales clerk who deals with customers, or a counter person in any service industry or organization that deals with the public. Consider:

*Yes, Mr. Jones, I can certainly understand that it seemed to be taking the service technician a long time to fix your cable TV. Isn't your new picture wonderful? We're so happy to be able to offer you this conversion at no charge.*

If you are a teacher who deals with parents, principals, and students, thinking on your feet saves time and sometimes a great deal of hassle:

*Yes, Mr. Smith, we should both be curious why Andrea didn't bring the sex-education-film notice home to you for a signature. Perhaps she can tell us what happened to it.*

Hunting for a job? Responding to interview questions beautifully is part of thinking on your feet (even if you're seated). Imagine how much better you'll feel when you realize that you never again have to respond to a question with a "no." Instead of having to say, "No, I don't know how to run an XR-7," you will be able to respond with enthusiasm: "I've used the XR-6 and am eager to learn the XR-7."

Does your job require you to answer questions frequently? Thinking on your feet quickly and correctly is the secret to success in that portion of your job. Answering well the first time solves problems, forestalls follow-up questions, and enables you to be more productive.

As a supervisor or manager, thinking on your feet will enable you to deflect hostile questions from subordinates, turning a potential conflict into a workable solution. The result: happier employees and a more harmonious work environment.

How are your employee relations? Do you remember to use those *One-Minute Manager*-type compliments, or do you think of them after you've gone back to your office. The techniques of thinking on your feet will help you share the special words at the right moment.

Do you tend to fly off the handle at people, wishing only a few minutes (or even seconds) later that you could take back what you blurted out, undo what you just did? When you can think on your feet, you will be less likely to put one of them in your mouth.

As a consumer do you sometimes get so irritated that you could scream? Would you rather find that what is coming out of your mouth is that "perfect" rejoinder that comes to mind just after you get back in the car or hang up the phone? Learn to think on your feet and those great responses will come at the appropriate time, not later. (It's hard to call someone later and declare, "*This* is what I wanted to say: 'Fix it first, and don't call me again until it's *right!*'")

Do you want more effective communications with other human beings? Do you want better relationships with them? Do you want to be poised and professional? These are the three attainable goals for people who think on their feet. You will discover many more applications to your own life as you read the examples and practice the techniques in this book.

### The "To Do" List

Before you go on to chapter 3, take a moment to jot down the main reasons why you want to think better on your feet. Write down several situations in which you would be happier if you responded better.

# CHAPTER 3
## About Questions

The first lesson is "About Questions." The more you know about questions, the easier it will be for you to answer those that are posed to you. Chances are excellent that you will know more about questions than most of those people who query you. If you happen to be asked an appropriate question in just the right pattern, you are fortunate. But if you are asked a question any old way, you will still be able to substitute the appropriate pattern as part of your answer (see chapter 5).

The English language has a variety of question patterns. Four basic patterns form most of the questions that people ask:

- yes-no questions
- closed information questions

- open information questions
- open-ended questions

The patterns move from structured or closed (yes-no) to unstructured or open (open-ended questions). At the structured end of the spectrum, questions seek information and facts; at the unstructured end, they seek opinions, feelings, or observations.

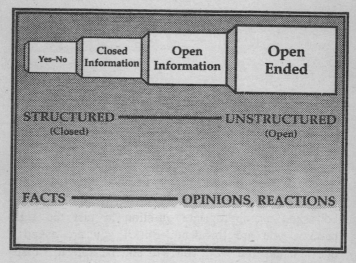

## Yes-No Question Patterns

The yes-no pattern creates a question that requests a direct response. These are examples of yes-no questions:

*Are you happy?*
*Is this the only color the suit comes in?*
*Did you finish my repairs?*
*Was the part ordered the day I called?*

*Do you have any houses for sale for under $80,000?*
*Was our service satisfactory?*

These questions begin with different forms (or tenses) of the verbs *to be*, *to have*, *to do*, and words such as *can*, *would*, *should*, and *will*.

Yes-no questions are the most used type of question. And because the answer can be a simple "yes" or "no," sometimes it is a good idea. Sometimes these questions are excellent; they are suited for those instances when you need direct or specific information and you are fairly certain that the individual has a direct response to give.

## Problems with Yes-No Patterns

Several problems exist with yes-no questions, however. These questions are called closed questions because they often "close" the dialogue between two people (see below). Another problem is that people are seldom satisfied with just a "yes" or "no"; they want/need/desire more information than that. The result is that the initial yes-no question is wasted, because a follow-up question is required. An information question can usually get both the yes or no and the supporting information at the same time.

A third difficulty is that questioners may feel hurt by the brusque or terse, simple answers they appear to request. It is difficult to put much expression or warmth into a one-syllable answer, as witnessed by the following exchange between an automobile owner and a service department employee:

JOHN: *Good morning. Is my car ready?*
NANCY: *No.*
JOHN (a bit peeved): *Well, when will it be ready?*
NANCY (now also a bit peeved): *It was scheduled for four o'clock, so I assume it will be ready by then.*

The yes-no question caused unnecessary tension in what can be a simple positive exchange:

JOHN: *Good morning. My car is scheduled to be done at four o'clock. I wonder if it just might be done early.*
NANCY: *It will be ready as scheduled, I'm sure. Would you like me to call you if it gets done before four o'clock?*
JOHN: *Yes, thanks, that would be nice of you.*

## Communication Involves a Contract

The most important difficulty with yes-no questions and answers is that you have cut off, or closed, the conversation. Think about it this way: successful communication—any conversation, social or business—involves an unspoken contract between the participating parties. This contract has two conditions: (1) both people want the communication to succeed, and (2) both people contribute to the communication. The result is a layering effect, a building of the information pool. Each listens and then adds to what the other has said. If either one does not want the conversation to succeed, all that person has to do is not add additional information, and the conversation will soon cease.

To illustrate this contract, notice what happens in the ritual social greeting:

JOHN: *Hi, Nancy.*
NANCY: *Hello, John.*

If neither party contributes beyond the ritual, the conversation is over. But consider this exchange:

JOHN: *Hi, Nancy. How are you?*
NANCY: *John, hi. It's good to see you. I'm fine. I love this weather!*
JOHN: *Me too. I'm planning to go hiking in the gorge this weekend. Do you hike?*

The layering of information has kept the conversation going smoothly and each has learned some additional information about the other. If you are a sales representative, consider how much rapport-building you have done with just two lines of conversation.

Yes-no questions do have a definite function in business and personal relationships. These direct questions are useful for taking care of routine details. They are also suited for those instances when you need specific information and are fairly certain that the customer, client, or co-worker has such a response to give. Yes-no questions are efficient in terms of time—a valuable resource for busy people.

## Closed Information Questions

Words such as *when*, *where*, *who*, and *what time* seek information by directing the responder—and the response—to a specific area:

*What time may we deliver your supplies?*
*Who will sign for the delivery?*
*What kind of system do you use?*

The response is apt to be as direct as the question:

*Friday after four o'clock would be perfect.*
*The purchasing manager.*
*A Zitox 204.*

When all that is wanted is precise information, this is the question pattern to use. It communicates exactly and saves time.

Because the answer can often be just one word, closed information questions can be almost as closed as yes-no questions:

ROB: *Where is the meeting?*
JIM: *My house.*
ROB: *Who is attending?*
JIM: *Just about everyone.*
ROB: *When is it?*
JIM: *Tomorrow.*

Not much layering being built here. It is difficult to develop any rapport. The seeker may get a strong feeling that the responder is not enjoying the conversation. Unless *just* information is required (and that simply isn't true with most of our conversational exchanges), these questions close the conversation and make rapport building difficult.

As a general rule, ask closed information questions

(1) when you are in a hurry and you know the other person is too; (2) when the conversation is with a person whom you know well, so goodwill does not need to be built. Avoid asking this type of question early in an interview or in a conversation with a new acquaintance or client, as the short responses might cut off the discussion too early. Avoid asking such blunt questions when the customer or responder seems intimidated, because they can sound like an interrogation.

## Open Information Questions

By contrast, the open information questions—*how, why,* and *what*—are the best for beginning conversations because each typically requires several words to answer it. Responders are encouraged to share more information than might be strictly necessary, to be open in their responses. Consider:

ALFRED: *What is the theme of the meeting?*
VALERIE: *It's "Safety Pays," the national convention's theme this year.*
ALFRED: *How can I help with the meeting?*
VALERIE: *You could bring the manuals with you. That would be a big help.*
ALFRED: *Why are you hosting it at your house?*
VALERIE: *We want a relaxed environment so that people won't feel threatened.*

Potentially important information is exchanged, and some room for warmth and concern is expressed.

Open information questions are formed with opening words and phrases that present larger areas for discussion while still providing some structure. Such phrases can also open up the communications and maintain structure: *What about benefits?* or, *How about the communications system?* or, *How do you feel about the goals?* You encourage longer responses and more information within a prescribed area of concern.

## Open-Ended Questions

These unstructured beginnings are often not questions at all, but the result is the same: (1) the responder is required to think through an answer and deliver it at some length; (2) the responder is given latitude to begin wherever he feels most comfortable, has the strongest feelings, or feels most secure. Phrases to use to get these open responses include *Tell me about . . .* , or *Describe . . .* , and *why* and *how*, when not focused. (Examples: *How are you feeling about this?* or, *Why did this happen?*)

Most of us need the chance to open up a bit, to search around in our minds for the words we wish to speak. Those who ask open-ended questions are recognizing people's occasional need to find a comfort level before becoming direct and specific. Open-ended questions are the most indirect questions. Such questions are designed to encourage people to think, to express opinions, and to share ideas, and they indicate that as the questioner you wish an open response.

More than that, open-ended questions encourage a fuller disclosure of information, of background, or of apprehensions than do a typical series of "get those facts first" questions. So, if you are a sales clerk, an outside sales rep, or are dealing with another person with whom you wish to establish rapport, these open-ended questions allow that to happen naturally.

When interviewing a potential customer, instead of starting out with "filling out the form" kinds of questions, try this:

*To begin, why don't you tell me about the kinds of services you offer and the needs you see.*

or

*First, would you describe your basic business operations for me?*

These open-ended questions establish a comfort level that enables both of you subsequently to deal more directly and completely. The open-ended approach may take longer, but the overall gain in rapport far outweighs the additional time commitment. With an open-ended beginning, you tell a client that he or she is important as a person and not just as an account number.

What comes from openness, of course, is much more than just the information you ask for. You gain insight into people's beliefs, habits, communication skills, levels of attention to detail—all good to know in establishing a satisfactory long-term relationship. The more unstructured the question, the more information you are likely to gain.

Unstructured questions are also used for less precise, but often more important, information. Your goal is to determine how someone feels about something, to discover what is on someone's mind (not something you can ask a specific question to discover). You also have an opportunity to draw people more actively into a conversation with open-ended questions.

As you think about answering questions, remember these patterns and their goals. If asked a yes-no question, on most occasions give more of an answer than is requested. However, if you do *not* want to enter into the contract, if it is a situation where you wish to send a signal that says, *I do not want to have a conversation with you*, you have that tool, too. Just say *yes* or *no* and stop.

If people seek precise facts, offer them and then stop, as long as you have assessed the situation and know there is no need to build rapport or goodwill.

When asked an open question, give a fuller response, but do not consider it an invitation to tell all you know on the subject. See chapter 11, "Delivery," for tips on how long you can safely respond to open-ended queries.

# CHAPTER 4

## About Answers . . . And Responses—Why a Response Is Usually Better Than an Answer

People tend to give answers in one of two ways: too long or too short. A too-short answer makes the seeker interrogate you to get all the information that is needed. A too-long answer (more common) turns out to be a small—or not so small—speech.

What's the solution? A *response:* the answer, plus one piece of support. The support may be a reason, a justification, a statistic, a quotation, a fact, or an opinion. The secret is to mention *just one* supporting item.

### How Much Information Should Be Given?

People often like to hear some depth with your answer, some justification, and you should supply it. But what do you do instead? If you are a short-answer person, you say

"Yes, usually," or "Sometimes that's true," or, "At six o'clock," and then close your mouth. The seeker must ask follow-up questions. Consider the following exchange between a club member and a professional speaker:

MARCIA: *Do you offer a special discount for nonprofit groups?*
CHELSEA: *Yes, usually.*
MARCIA: *Well, would we be eligible for it?*
CHELSEA: *You might be. It depends.*
MARCIA: *What does it depend on?*
CHELSEA: *It depends on several things.*
MARCIA: *Could you give me an example?*
CHELSEA: *Who you are going to invite, for one thing.*
MARCIA: *Only our members are invited. No outsiders or spouses.*
CHELSEA: *Then you would be eligible for a discount.*

That's a frustrating conversation. The seeker is apt to become irritated because of the shortness of the answers, even though she is partly to blame because of the yes-no pattern she chose. The responder will begin to feel as if she is being interrogated and become hostile, even though she is causing the difficulty with her short answers and lack of any support. She is making the seeker pull the information out of her.

MARCIA: *Do you offer a special discount for nonprofit groups?*
CHELSEA: *Yes, I am able to offer one to certain groups. If the audience is solely members, where there is no commercial gain or profit involved, a discount is possible.*
MARCIA: *Wonderful! We do qualify, then.*

The contrast is startling. Three exchanges instead of ten save a great deal of time. Even though the seeker used a yes-no question, the responder answered more fully. The seeker is pleased with the information she received, and the responder's tone of voice is undoubtedly better, as she is conveying positive news in a positive manner.

## What If You *Want* to Give More Information?

It's fine to suggest that you should give only one piece of support, the main piece if possible. But what if you have lots more wonderful information that you are just dying to give? The approach is the same: Give just one main piece of support... but build in a clue that indicates that you have more details to add, if the seeker wishes to hear them. The goal in general conversation is to let the seeker know, so that he or she may control the extent of the exchange.

Why let the seeker control? you may well ask. First, the person asking the questions is always the one in control. The second reason is less obvious. Remember the premise at the beginning of this chapter, that most of us tend to give a small speech when asked a question. We do that because we like the sound of our own voice, we are enthused about the topic, and we have lots of information to share. However, none of these reasons is a *good* reason for telling the seeker more than he or she wants to know.

The only good reason to give real depth of information in general conversation is that the seeker wants it. Building in a clue enables you to respond specifically but briefly, at the same time letting the seeker know that all he or she has to do is ask and you will gladly provide more.

Words such as *main, primary, most essential,* and *major* all provide that clue: *The main reasons for the change . . . ; The most important factor in our decision . . . ; The primary goal . . .* All the seeker needs to do is say, *What are some of the other reasons?* or, *What else figured into your decision?* You add more information and you add it confidently because the seeker wishes it. You are not worried about being a bore or losing the seeker's attention. You maintain your credibility, your poise, and your professional demeanor.

Often, though, the seeker will be perfectly satisfied with just the answer and the main reason. What is the result? A question and a response, with no time wasted and no fear of boring another with excess enthusiasm or information. The communication exchange is successful, and the relationship stays positive.

## The Basic Communications Exchange

There is another, more compelling reason to give a response with the clue built in for additional information. That reason centers on the nature of the basic communications discussed in chapter 3: the contract between two people that requires both to want the conversation to continue and to add information to it. If you respond to a question with five (or more) minutes of your great knowledge, wisdom, or opinion, the other person—the other half of your conversation—is left out. He is waiting, patiently or less than patiently, for you to draw a breath so that he can get back into the conversation.

In other words, you are giving a monologue rather than having a dialogue with the other person. The exchange of information brought out by a question, a response, a comment, another question, and another response is a natural exchange. Both people are participating, contributing to an ongoing communication process. Both the initial seeker and the initial responder are involved (which will not be true for long if you give your speech without interruption).

The question-and-answer format has turned into a conversation. Whether you are selling, buying, offering service, or asking for service, the transaction will nearly always go better if it becomes a conversation. Rapport is built, confidence grows, and trust begins to be established.

That is why, even if you are trying to make a sale or satisfy a customer's problem—and you wish to be in control—you will generally have more success if you give a response, with a clue, so that the conversation can build.

A final reason for building in a clue is that it reminds your brain to stop sending words to your mouth after it sends the main point, the most essential strategy, or the key to success. I can virtually guarantee you that if you say, *The most important reason we selected this firm is that we know we can work with them,* your brain will understand that it should send no more words down the line. I've seen real motormouths learn to be concise by mastering and using this one simple tool.

## Do You Have to Answer the Question at All?

The answer to that question is, not necessarily. Most people answer every question they are asked, just out of habit; that's often not the appropriate thing to do. Nowhere is it written that you must answer every question asked of you. No one forces words out of your mouth. And some people answer every question just exactly the way it was asked, which is an even less appropriate thing to do. (See chapter 7, "Getting a Better Question to Answer.")

Even though you can answer, you may not want to give the exact answer. You may wish to give only part of the information; or some other piece of information may be more appropriate. As the holder of the information, you should decide what to answer and how to answer it.

### Points to Remember

Give a response: the answer plus one main piece of support. Build in a clue to stop yourself from talking too long and to show that you would like a follow-up question. To build good relations, have conversations, not question-and-answer periods.

### The "To Do" List

Take a moment to think about the people with whom you interact on a daily basis. Do you give them appropriate responses, do you give a speech at every opportunity, or do you just answer their questions and stop? Think about this: You might improve relations with some of those people—at work or at home—if you respond with more thought, if you treat them the same way you treat a customer or client.

# CHAPTER 5
## Responding to Easy Questions—The Kind You Can and Want to Answer

How many times have you slapped your thigh and thought, *That's what I should have said!* two minutes after you had hung up the phone? How often have you said to yourself, *If only I'd thought of that earlier?* What you realize is that most of the time the appropriate response was there in your mind all the time just waiting to be spoken. But you blurted out the first thing that got to your tongue, not the best thing you could have said in response.

There is a secret to responding successfully to all types of questions and it is easy to remember: Put your brain in gear before you put your mouth in gear. The technique of buying time to think about what you want to say is a simple one.

What do you do with those few precious seconds that you buy? Organize your thoughts. Failure to pause to organize and to activate your brain is what causes you to strike your forehead in disbelief at what just came out of your mouth. Sometimes it seems like someone else is talking, doesn't it?

With easy questions you can frequently buy enough time to organize just with silence. *Silence?* Yes. Simply remain silent until your brain has had the few seconds it needs to find the appropriate information. Your brain is a powerful computing device; it needs only a minute amount of time to sort through the probable responses to get the one you want to utter. The seeker does not expect you to open your mouth the second hers is closed. In fact, you generally have four or five times as long to organize as you feel you have before you begin speaking.

What if the time you can naturally buy with silence is not enough? The other basic time-buying strategy is to repeat the question. You can do that in one of two ways: repeat it as a question or repeat it as part of your response. Either way, your mouth will be able to repeat those words easily, giving your brain a few additional seconds to come up with what will follow.

If you repeat the question as a question, nonverbal gestures and intonation are both important. Suppose the question is, "Why have your prices been raised again?"

You pause, perhaps raising your eyebrows slightly, and repeat: *Why have the prices gone up? . . . A slight raise was necessary because the cost of paper supplies doubled in the last six months.* (Notice the addition of the word *slight* and the change to the neutral "*the* price" rather than the personal "*your* prices." You have succeeded in diffusing the negative intention of the question while at the same time answering directly and honestly.)

With the identical question, the response that repeats the question as part of the answer is, *It was necessary to raise the prices slightly because the cost of paper supplies doubled in the last six months*. The same diffusing of the negative implication occurs here.

Naturally, you must not adopt either approach as your only one. That's why there are many alternative approaches in chapters 6 through 10.

## How Can You Be Successful?

There are five basic steps for success in responding to all questions:

1. listen—pay attention to what's been said
2. pause to organize
3. repeat the question
4. give the one main support
5. *stop*—don't end on an excuse

## Listen—Pay Attention to What's Been Said

This step is important for many reasons. First, you do not wish to feel foolish because you missed some point or, worse, repeated what someone else has said. Second, if you have heard what's been said previously you have a chance to reinforce a key point that someone has made. Third, you have the opportunity to correct what you believe to be a misstatement by another. Fourth, you can compliment another by being able to say, *I agree with*

*Joan;* or, *Jim's point about that was a good one.* Next, you have the opportunity to read the nonverbal messages being sent. These sometimes support the message but sometimes send a conflicting message that you must consider. Finally, you can sum up or paraphrase aspects that have been covered, not only buying more time but improving the total communications situation. And you will sound great.

Even if you are conversing with only one other person, you can accomplish a great deal more, with more professionalism and confidence, when you know exactly what has been said—not just parts of it.

## Pause to Organize

This is the essential time-buying phase that ensures that you say exactly what you want to say, even with easy questions. You also look and sound poised and in control when you deliberate for a few seconds, especially if the question was meant to be a complex one. There is power in that silence.

## Repeat the Question

Remember that you can repeat the question two ways, as a question or as part of your answer. If the question is, *How long have you been speaking for money, Marian?* my response choices are: (1) *I've been a professional speaker for nearly twenty years;* or (2) *How long have I been a professional speaker? I got my first paid job twenty years ago.* (Notice I rephrased the question slightly to upgrade it.)

It is important to repeat the question when speaking with one other person and it is mandatory to repeat it when speaking in front of or with a group. Here are four of the reasons:

- Buy time to think. It's easy to say the words of the question while your brain is busily searching for what to insert after the question.
- Help your brain to focus on the topic. My clients tell me that their responses are better virtually every time if they repeat the question.
- Refocus a hostile or negative question with subtlety. For example, if the question is, *Why are your fees so high?* you could refocus the question slightly in your response, *Fees reflect both my experience and your guarantee of satisfaction.*
- Clarify the question.

In addition, recognize these two facts: (1) the answer is only part of the information you wish to convey; the question plus the answer is the complete information; (2) when you are part of a group (whether the speaker, a panel member, or a member of the audience), you enable everyone to hear the question. It's frustrating to be in an audience and hear these three answers from the speaker:

*Yes, I agree.*
*I don't think that's applicable in this case.*
*That's true. I couldn't have phrased it better myself.*

## Give the One Main Support

To give a response, rather than just an answer, add one piece of support to the answer and then stop. Most of the time you will satisfy the seeker, enabling him or her to go on to the next topic. If you *wish* to say more, build in the clue word *main*, or *major*, or *primary*. If the seeker wishes more information, the follow-up question will be naturally asked.

*Note:* Giving one main item of support is a rule of thumb and a reminder to people not to give a speech. You will decide in some situations to give two reasons, or even three. When you give more than one reason, include oral guidelines just as you do in a speech. The oral guidelines follow your main sentence; they are phrased to include the specific number of points you will make: ... *and there are three major reasons for my decision.*
Here's a response with oral guidelines:

> *Yes, I do support his decision to purchase this system. My decision is based on three criteria: the cost is within our budget, the quality is high, and the system interfaces with the equipment in the downtown offices.*

A word of caution: Remember that most of us have a great deal more information—and tend to give it—than people want.

## Stop—Don't End on an Excuse

This step is vital whether you wish to maintain your professional poise or to appear to be an assertive consumer, a responsible teacher, or any confident individual. So often people give a fine response, with just the right amount of information and just the appropriate tone, and then blow it all by babbling on beyond the finish or by shrugging at the end. If you can't figure out a way to stop, try this trick: Repeat the essence of the question as a close: *So that's why we decided to stop the project.*

Ask your family or your colleagues to monitor you to see if you have developed one of those two habits (because that is often all it is—a habit). Ask them if you sometimes add a verbal excuse such as, *But I don't know if that's what you want you know;* or *But I haven't really studied that aspect yet;* or *I really don't have a strong opinion on that.*

## Points to Remember

To respond to questions that you wish to answer directly, give your answer, add the main support, and stop. That's all there is to it.

## The "To Do" List

Write down three or four basic questions that you have to respond to frequently. These are apt to be questions about your basic service or product, about your organization or business. Practice a response—the answer, plus one main piece of support for each of the questions. Practice building in a clue, so that you can establish a conversation rather than give a sales pitch.

# CHAPTER 6
# Responding to Difficult Questions

What makes questions difficult to answer? Four categories describe the majority of difficult questions:

- questions that are long, complex, confusing, or not well thought out (chapter 7)
- questions that are inappropriate to the time and place and questions deliberately designed to intimidate you (chapter 8)
- questions phrased in a negative way (chapter 9)
- questions that should be addressed to someone else (chapter 10)

What to do? How can you retain the same calm, poised, professional (or personal) demeanor when you've just been thrown a curve? How can you make the seeker feel satisfied? The difficulties and specific solutions are discussed in detail in each of the next four chapters. But first, general tips.

## Again, Give a Response, Not an Answer

First of all, use the skills you acquired and practiced in responding to routine questions. Use the same basic tools:

- pay attention and listen carefully
- pause to organize
- repeat the question
- support your answer briefly

The new tool is this: give an *indirect* response instead of a direct one.

To give an indirect response is to answer inductively: give the explanation first, then follow with the answer. The result is a cushioned explanation. To illustrate: If your mate asks you why you are late getting home, your cushioning, indirect response might be:

> *After our planning meeting, the boss wanted to talk briefly about my role in the project; she suggested that we go over to The Nest. It was so crowded that we had trouble getting waited on. So what should have been a twenty-minute meeting lasted more than an hour.*

(Sure beats, "I had a drink with my boss," doesn't it?)

## Buy Time to Think

However indirectly you wish to respond, you must still give some substance in most instances. So these responses require even more thought and planning than easy responses. The secret is the same: buy time to think. Repeating the question will sometimes do the trick, as it does with easy questions. Another advantage of repeating the question is that if you repeat the words, you will be more likely to give the appropriate answer, which is sometimes better than giving just the right answer. Assume that you're a management consultant who has just finished making a presentation to the executive committee of a company. You have proposed installing a computerized internal control system that would do a better job of keeping track of the company's inventory. The first question comes directly at you from the president: *Will this system you are recommending guarantee that we won't have any more shortages in inventory?*

Unless you buy time to think, your candid response is apt to be, *No, I can't guarantee that.* That may be the right answer, but it certainly isn't the appropriate one. Buying time by repeating the question (and thus hearing it again) should enable you to say *The question is, "Can I guarantee you'll have no more shortages?" This is, after all, a system, and all systems are fallible. But it is the best inventory system available. I can guarantee that this system will be a tremendous improvement over your present one.*

Learn to repeat just the heart of the question. This tactic shortens the total response time and focuses the listener on the key element of your response. The next question comes from the vice president of finance: *You just said that the cost for this fancy computerized system is over $10,000. That's a lot of money. I know there are cheaper systems on the market. I think we don't need such a fancy system.*

Repeating the heart of his comment, you say, *Why do you need to buy the 2000D series? Because it is by far the best value for the money.* You are also minimizing the negative here. (See chapter 8 for more ideas on omitting the negative.)

## Buy Time with a Pause

More often than you might believe, you can buy enough time to plan your response with silence—just by pausing. Well-timed pauses can be powerful and purposeful devices in any verbal situation, and responding to questions is no exception. A pause can be considered verbal white space, time surrounding a key idea in the same way white space in an advertisement surrounds and thus emphasizes a key point. A pause also commands attention for what is to follow in the same way that a colon does in writing when introducing a list.

Finally, a pause prevents fillers such as *and uh, er, y'know,* and *uh.* These nonwords come out of mouths as mental static when brains have not yet become activated. When the brain goes blank, it's best to turn off the sound!

## Buy Time with a Nonverbal Gesture

A few extra seconds can be gained by a nonverbal gesture. Indicate that you have heard the question and are preparing a response. Such a gesture might be a nod, a slight lift of the hand, or a smile (but never a grimace). People who ask difficult questions usually know they are doing so; some will appreciate your thoughtfulness in responding. Too, if you begin to speak the instant the seeker closes his mouth, you sometimes sound as if you have a set answer ready to pull out. People feel that they deserve a personal response. Your taking time to think is seen as a compliment; you are saying—nonverbally—*I think your question is a good one, and I'm going to give you a well-thought-out response*.

### Points to Remember

When asked a question you feel discomfort about, your basic strategy is the same as with easy questions: buy time to compose your thoughts. You want to have confidence that the appropriate response gets from your brain to your mouth.

### The "To Do" List

Chapters 7 through 10 involve techniques for answering difficult questions. Before you read these tips, write down some of the difficult questions you tend to be asked. They may be questions you do not like to answer, should not answer, or cannot answer. Consult your list of difficult questions as you read the next four chapters.

# CHAPTER 7

# Get a Better Question to Answer

Often a question is virtually unanswerable because of the kind of question it is—long, complicated, multifaceted, or obscure. People ask such difficult questions for many reasons. Sometimes the seeker simply hasn't thought out the question well enough in advance; the result is a vague question, whether long or short. Don't try to answer a vague question, because there is no way you can please the seeker. Get a better question.

Sometimes the seeker does not know enough about the topic to phrase a question well. This is a problem especially when people ask questions about new information or products. Ask a question that introduces two aspects, requiring them to choose which they are interested in. You can educate them and get a better question to answer at the same time.

At other times, the questioner has lots on her mind and

she tries to get it all into one question; the result is a rambling question with many facets. It's foolish to try to figure out which part of the question is most important to the questioner. And it's equally foolish to try to work all the answers into one response. Get a better question.

At still other times, the seeker is trying to stump you, either because he has it in for you or he just likes to sound off—or show off. People who deliberately ask difficult questions believe that by doing so they will pin you right to the wall. Don't let that happen. Get a better question.

## How Can You Get a Better Question?

Here are five basic ways to get a better question to respond to:

- ask to have the question repeated
- ask a question of your own
- ask for clarification
- ask for a definition
- clarify or define a point yourself

## Ask to Have the Question Repeated

One of the problems with questions, as discussed in chapter 3, is that people don't spend much time thinking about how they wish to ask them. That is a big problem when you are attempting to present a poised response. When you ask a seeker to repeat his question, he gets a chance to hear it. He is usually glad to repeat it, to have another chance to sound more knowledgeable. He will frequently begin again with, *What I meant was . . .* or, *What I was trying to say was . . .* In most instances you will get a better question to answer. It will typically be shorter, more specific, and more focused. It is often no longer a difficult question but an easy one.

However, if it does come out exactly the same way the second time, you can be virtually certain that the person is indeed trying to pin you to the wall. The delivery is apt to be more emphatic and more caustic, but the words won't change.

Consider this exchange between a taxpayer and his state representative at the end of a campaign talk:

> *You say you're against more taxes. Tell me this, why have you kept voting "yes" every single time a tax package has come up before the House the last two years that you've been pretending to represent the wishes of this district?*

It is important to buy a bit of time to think about your record, so your first response is:

> *I'm sorry, I couldn't hear all your question; it's a bit noisy in here. Would you repeat it, please?*

The taxpayer responds in a pained tone, louder and slower:

> *I SAID, "You say you're against more taxes. . . . Why have you been voting 'yes'? . . ."*

You get the idea: word for word, with more emphasis so everyone can hear it this time.

If the taxpayer is seriously asking the question, he is more apt to repeat his question this way:

> If you're against more taxes, why do you keep voting for more?

Either way, what have you gained? Let's take as the first assumption that you generally do hear the question. You get the drift. Having it repeated—whether you get a better question or not—buys your brain the additional seconds to figure out what it will send out of your mouth when the repeat is finished. Even if the taxpayer is trying to pin you down, you still have a better opportunity to respond with some degree of success than if you tried to have a go at it the first time.

## Ask a Question of Your Own

It is virtually always legitimate to ask a question of your own in response to a seeker's inquiry. You are attempting to clarify what the seeker wants to know. This approach is especially important if the question is many-faceted or vague. Do not lose sight of the fact that your goal is successful communication with another person. There is little point to responding with information that the seeker is not seeking. In addition, you lay yourself open to the sarcasm of, *Well, that's interesting, but it isn't what I asked you*, or *My question was about 1990, not 1991*.

Often your goal in asking a question of your own is to get the seeker to focus the question more, to narrow it to a more specific time frame, a specific product, a precise problem. And he or she usually will.

## Ask for Clarification

Lack of clarity in an inquiry often means lack of clarity in the questioner's mind. There is little point in your trying to respond brilliantly, because the answer will not please the seeker anyway. He doesn't know what it is he wants. Get a better question by having the seeker clarify (to himself and to you) what it is he wants to know. Simply say, *Could you clarify what you mean by excess?* or, *Training is a complex subject; can you be a bit more specific?*

This is a refinement on asking a question of your own, but it forces the seeker, not you, to do the clarification. One of your best approaches is a choice or option question: *Do you want the figures for 1990 or 1991?* or, *Is your concern with the product itself or with the warranty?* or, *Do you mean the delivery or the postsale service?* Again, you wish to give the seeker the information he is looking for. Assuming that the information is appropriate for him to have, forcing him to clarify the scope of the question will help you do exactly that. Frequently it becomes an easy question to answer, too.

Lack of clarity in questions is a problem at home as well as in business. Consider this teenager talking to her parent about restrictions:

TEEN: *I don't see why I have to be in at midnight when nobody else does; they can all come home whenever the party is over. It's not easy to get a ride early and I sure don't want you to show up there. I'd be so embarrassed I'd just crawl under a rock. Why do you have to come?*

PARENT: *Well, I know that other kids in your group do have curfews too. I was talking to Martha Jones at the store and she told me that Rich has to be home by midnight. And so there will be other parents there picking up their kids. You shouldn't be embarrassed about having parents. Everybody has parents.*

What a terrible exchange! The teen did not have her real problem identified, and the parent did not help her identify it. The parent undoubtedly did not know exactly what the real problem was either. If the parent had helped her daughter to clarify what she really wanted to ask, the second part of the conversation could have gone like this:

PARENT: *Are you more concerned about the time or about my coming to pick you up?*

TEEN: *Well . . . I guess it's that you'd come up to the door and embarrass me by saying something stupid in front of all my friends.*

PARENT: *Let's do this: I'll arrive at midnight and wait in the car for you. If you come out within ten minutes and look for the car, I won't even need to get out. That will please both of us. Okay?*

It's a better exchange, isn't it? The parent has not nagged her daughter by bringing up a lot of baggage that isn't relevant to the moment. The daughter has been able to say what it is that truly bugs her. Each can feel good rather than bad, and their relationship is improved.

## Ask for a Definition

Anytime you are discussing information or concepts that contain words that might have more than one interpretation, it is important to be sure all of you are using those words in the same way. Abstract concepts, projects in the design stage, theories of finance, inventory methods, sales approaches—all these and many other topics can be defined by the seeker to make you certain that you and he or she are using the words the same way. Especially with abstractions and theories, you may well expound at some length, happily and confidently, only to be greeted at the close of your response with, *What are you talking about?* (or worse).

Your punctured ego will have difficulty getting back to normal size, resulting in your less-than-poised performance for at least the next few exchanges. You can avoid potential deflated egos by asking the seeker to define the word that can lead to trouble. It is easy to say, *Could you define "value-added" as you perceive it?* or, *Would you give me your definition of "moral" in this context?* You will both be in the same ballpark as you begin your response. Remember, it is not necessary that you agree with the definition, only that you understand how the seeker is using the word. If you do disagree, part of your response may be in defining it yourself.

If by chance the seeker has asked the tough question to

put you on the spot, you are gently but firmly putting him on that spot—all without a smudge on your poise. If he cannot define the term, which is sometimes the case with troublemakers, he will likely mumble something and withdraw. No more difficult question to answer.

If he can and does define it, wonderful. You have two advantages now: first, a clearer understanding of how the inquiry is focused, and second, more time to get your response ready, during the moments the definition is being readied and verbalized.

## Clarify or Define a Point Yourself

As the responder you also have the option to clarify the question as you heard it or to define a concept. Some people believe they can maintain better control if they refocus the question in their response. The down side of clarifying an inquiry yourself is that you may not clarify to the satisfaction of the seeker. Your response is also longer if you do your own clarification or definition. It is easy to run on too long in this preliminary material and not get to the answer. However, that in itself can be a successful avoidance tactic. (See chapter 8.)

How might this definition process begin your response?

STOCKHOLDER: *It seems to us that you just keep spending money. Why are you doing that instead of giving us dividends?*

CEO: *If by "spending money" you are referring to the new computerized inventory system we installed, I'm delighted to tell you that the system has improved our shipment time by 40 percent, giving us a net increase in profits of 30 percent. You will see some of that profit increase in your dividends this year.*

If you use the clarification approach, consider this exchange:

PARENT: *When I look at my kid's class schedule, all I see are educational classes. Why aren't you giving him stuff to help him get a job?*

PRINCIPAL: *I take the word "educational" to mean classes such as history and English. The core of our curriculum is dictated by the State Board of Education, and certainly those classes are part of that core. But in English class, for example, teachers are including some business-letter writing as assignments. Those will help your son get jobs and also do solid work in his profession, whatever it is.*

It is tempting occasionally to begin this way: *By "educational" do you mean history and English?* in order to let the seeker confirm your clarification. Sometimes this approach is helpful, to be certain the conversation is on track. However, there is a great problem inherent in letting the seeker back into the lead: he may launch into his favorite speech about what's wrong with education, or he may ask yet another question. In most instances he will at least confuse the issue and give you a more difficult arena in which to respond. You want to respond to this question, clearly and with poise, before you are hit with some other onslaught.

## Points to Remember

Getting a better question to answer will alleviate many seemingly difficult question situations, turning most of them into easy questions—the kind you can and want to answer.

# CHAPTER 8
# Hedging, But Still in Control

The second category of difficult questions contains those that are inappropriate and those with hidden agendas. The solution: hedge. "To hedge" simply means to answer indirectly, or to refuse to commit oneself. Chapter 6 discussed basic indirect responses. This indirect approach is especially necessary with questions you can but do not want to answer directly. For various reasons, you decide that it is not appropriate to give the requested information. People frequently ask questions that are either inappropriate or—let's be candid—ignorant (read *ignorant* in its true definition: "showing lack of knowledge"). These folks probably mean well, but they do not realize that their query puts something at risk: confidential information, nonpublic facts, private estimates, prices, and so on. These people are not necessarily at fault; however, the problem remains, for you, to sound poised and credible while not disclosing the confidential information.

Occasionally you may be tempted to simply say, *That's none of your business*. You ought not to, unless you have beautiful control of your voice and intonation. It is possible to say, *This information is classified,* or *Those figures have not been released yet*. Tone of voice is important with those responses too; and you must be careful to give such a seeker the chance to save face. No one wishes to be embarrassed because of lack of knowledge. If the seeker happens to be someone significant to your work or your life, it is particularly important to give an appropriate response to that inappropriate question. That response is apt to be indirect, or hedged.

There are also people who know very well that the information they seek is privileged. They ask the question anyway; they like to see you squirm. Do the same cautions apply to these jerks? Yes, usually. While it is tempting to put those kind of people down with a witty one-liner, don't you find that such poor judgment often comes back to haunt you? That old geezer whom you made the object of your biting sarcasm turns out to be the new majority stockholder. The smart young thing whom you put in her place with a witty quip is the daughter of your biggest donor. It costs you nothing to remain professional, and it might cost you a great deal to lose your cool or give in to a whim.

## Tactics for Hedging Professionally

There are four basic approaches to choose from when seeking to respond indirectly in these situations:

- respond to one aspect of the question
- refocus the question
- "discuss" the question
- build a bridge between the inappropriate question and an appropriate response

Delivery is the key to success when employing any of these hedging tactics. Many people have such poor delivery when they try to respond indirectly that their audience is clearly aware that they are hedging and is put off by it. Such need not be the case. Knowing that the indirect approach is the appropriate one should give you confidence to carry it off. (See chapter 11 for special tips on delivery.)

## Respond to One Aspect of the Question

With questions that fall into the difficult category, one common problem is that there are a number of aspects that appear to need to be addressed. In this case, the problem becomes the solution: Pick the one aspect you want to answer and form your response around it. Ignore the rest. If your response has met the criteria discussed earlier, chances are that you will have satisfied the seeker. Remember that people ask questions for many reasons other than to get information. They want to hear you talk, to measure your poise, and to get your slant. A many-faceted question is frequently the result of someone not knowing exactly what to ask, or even exactly what he seeks. A solid, positive response on one aspect, with some specific support and delivered with a confident tone, will satisfy many situations.

What if one solid aspect does not satisfy the seeker? Suppose he comes back with, *Well, that's interesting, but you didn't talk about the stock option.* Are you hurt? No. You did hear that part too, and your brain undoubtedly gave it a bit of attention. So your second response will nearly always be better than your first one. You can also ask to have that part rephrased, buying yourself even more time to deal with the appropriate material. Consider this exchange between a boss and her secretary:

SECRETARY: *Last week you said that we could talk about the financial and growth opportunities for me here at XYZ Corp. Tell me about the training program. Am I eligible for the promotion plan? And what are the rumors I hear about the stock options available for management and not staff?*

BOSS: *This is a good time to talk about those opportunities, because I've just finished the new employee brochure. You are eligible for the training program now, and for the promotion plan after you have been here one year. The training agenda will be available in my office whenever it gets back from the printer.*

SECRETARY: *Well, that helps me, but you didn't talk about the stock options.*

BOSS: *What specific question did you have about the stock options?*

SECRETARY: *I wondered how it works and whether I'm eligible.*

BOSS: *It's based on a formula of years of service, plus*

*other variables in salary scale. The professional training and the promotion plan are designed exclusively for staff; the stock option is, at this time, available only for management.*

## Refocus the Question

When a question is directed toward material that is confidential or that you simply do not wish to share, you can refocus on a less restricted aspect. Your approach should be to take one word from the question (usually not the main topic word) that you are willing to discuss and build a strong, supported response around it.

Consider this question from a parent to his son's high school counselor:

> *I just can't understand why my son isn't doing better in school. He's got a good mind, he generally does his homework, he doesn't miss classes too often—he tells me—and he gets along okay with most of his teachers. Why is he not passing?*

Examine this question carefully. The counselor does not want to say that John has such a rotten attitude that none of his teachers can reach him, that his homework—when done—is sloppy and incomplete, and that he's missed so many classes that he's behind in three. The counselor may need to say those things at some point in the conversation, but he will want to deal with them one at a time. Trying to respond to all of them at the beginning of the conference would be inappropriate for many reasons:

(1) the response becomes a speech because each criticism must be supported; (2) the parent is listening rather than contributing; (3) the parent is put on the defensive, having his child attacked; (4) the parent is not having his support enlisted. Here's the appropriate response from the counselor:

> *John* does *have a good mind, Mr. Jones, and when he wants to use it, he can do work at the higher range of the class. He needs to decide that it's important to use his mind in every class. How do you think you might be able to help him decide to put that fine mind to work more often?*

The counselor's goals are to keep the dialogue going, to avoid having to say all negative things right up front, and to enlist the parent in the solution rather than placing him on the defensive. All of these can be accomplished by: (1) buying time to think, so that the appropriate thing is said, rather than the correct thing; (2) using an indirect approach, to soften what in this case is a mostly negative situation; and (3) employing the strategy of refocusing the question as the pattern for the response.

## "Discuss" the Question

Frequently people ask what sound like difficult questions, when all they really want is general information. I remember a question-and-answer session in an audience of Washington and Oregon businesspeople. The person fielding the questions was an assistant in one state's

Office of Economic Development. One question was, *Why don't Oregon and Washington cooperate more in economic development?*

That sounds like a real zinger, doesn't it? The responder was a pro; his opener was that more cooperation went on than was apparent. He mentioned one or two projects, went on to talk about various reasons that it didn't happen more (including competition), and closed with, *But I've really discussed your question, haven't I? I didn't answer it.* This close was accompanied by a charming smile.

It was a classic response. Of course he just discussed it, because (1) that was all he could do—that type of question has no answer, and (2) that's exactly what the seeker—and the rest of the audience—wanted. The better question would have been, *Please talk about the opportunities and problems of cooperation between our two states.* But as a speaker you don't often get the better question, so you respond to what's asked in what you feel is the appropriate way. Many times a discussion is that appropriate way.

Delivery counts here too. The responder who is poised and in control has no trouble with the charming smile and warm tone that the end of this response needs.

## Building a Bridge Between the Inappropriate Question and the Appropriate Response

A bridging response is a variation of the refocusing tactic. It is more versatile—and more difficult to carry off. Bridging enables you to move from what the seeker asked to what you want to talk about even if you can't find a key word of hers to use as your focus. The key here is obvious: The bridge must be strong enough to be a logical transition between the material of the question and your response material. If the bridge is not strong, it sounds as if you are faking it. A successful bridging response is a beautiful piece of professional speaking; a poor one sticks out for a mile.

The easiest way to construct the bridge is to briefly acknowledge what the seeker said and go on quickly from there. Here's a bridge:

UNCONVINCED PROSPECTIVE CLIENT: *I don't know. Your price is substantially above those of your competition. It's not going to be easy for me to convince my board to pay that much more.*
RESPONDER: *You're right that price is important, Jack, but quality is even more important, because you're looking at an investment, not just a purchase. You expect longer product life and you will get it. You expect a refinement of features and this model has them. Quality is the key.*

Another successful bridge:

Q: *Why aren't we sending more money to the XYZ project? It's a good project.*
A: *Yes, it's a good project. But money's only one issue here. The critical issue here is change.*

One more example:

Q: *I'm concerned about the amount of wheat that we're*

*sending to that country. Why are we selling to our*
*adversaries?*

A: *That's certainly one area of concern. But of even*
*greater concern are our own farmers; we must . . .*

You get the idea: Agree that something said is valid, true,
or of concern, and agree with it if you can, then move
quickly to the greater concern or more important issue
you want to talk about.

You may be more familiar with this tactic than any of
the others. Listen to the news conferences of elected or
appointed officials and candidates for good and not-so-
good examples. If the bridge was well built, you either
won't recognize it, or you will discover what happened
later, after you've replayed the dialogue in your mind. A
poor bridge is easy to spot: Everyone's reaction is apt to
be, *Give us a break! The question was about Iraq; how*
*did you get to South Africa?*

This tactic requires more practice than most others.
But when handled with a poised, confident style it is a
lifesaver, especially in those situations in which you
have an agenda and must get it covered. It's also
helpful for those whose dealings require talking a great
deal without giving much away. If you need this kind
of response you will soon see its application to your
area of expertise.

### Points to Remember

Do not be embarrassed by the need to hedge. Recognize that it is a legitimate manner of responding to

inappropriate questions and an acceptable approach for questions you cannot answer. Your hedge should be successful if you approach it with confidence. See chapter 11 for delivery tips to enhance that confidence.

# CHAPTER 9

# Responding with Positive Words to Negative Questions

Another category of difficult questions is those that people phrase in a negative way. It is usually disastrous to repeat either their negative words or their negative tone. Your goal is to respond so that the focus of the question itself becomes positive.

Negative questions, of course, include words such as *don't, can't, wouldn't, shouldn't*. Consider the parent whose query is, *Why can't my son read?* The teacher who can think on her feet simply turns both the question and the response into a positive encounter. This tactic not only defuses an angry parent, but it restores goodwill to the conversation and finds a solution to the problem. Here's one such turn-around:

PARENT: *Why can't my son read?*
TEACHER: *I'm glad that you're concerned about Jack's*

*reading level. One important thing you can do to help him is to read to him at home.*

Another possible response might be:

TEACHER: *I'm concerned about Jack's reading level too. Reading aloud to him at home would help him develop an interest in books. His skills will improve quickly when he becomes interested.*

When responding, the teacher used these techniques: (1) repeat the question as part of the answer; (2) change the negative concept *can't read* to a neutral *reading level.* This particular response also involves a tip discussed in the last chapter—refocusing the question.

## Who Ask These Kinds of Questions

People who phrase their questions in negative words are usually those who had an expectation that was not met. Some are disappointed or hostile; some have deadlines that have not been met (these are likely to be customers or clients); others have had a request turned down by someone (these are apt to be subordinates). Your first task is to identify what the expectation was, then give the seeker an explanation. Avoid increasing his or her hostility or disappointment. You can manage this feat quite easily if you remember not to go along with either the negative tone or the negative words.

Other people who ask negative questions are those

who, having failed to get what they wanted, feel they have no real recourse. These include subordinates, students of all ages, and children. It is important to avoid buying into the negative with them, too. Consider the high school student whose complaint is, *Why don't I ever get an "A" on a paper?* The response is too often apt to be, *Because you don't follow directions.*

The better response turns the negative into a positive and conveys the same answer, while giving a compliment:

TEACHER: *You know the information. You can earn an "A" on a paper if you follow the directions of the assignment.*

or:

TEACHER: *Following the directions of the assignment will get you an "A" every time if you know the material as well as you knew this material.*

Maybe the question is directed to a parent:

CHILD: *Why can't I have a computer? Everybody else has one.*
PARENT: *You can earn the money to buy a computer by shoveling snow for the neighbors this winter.*

## Points to Remember

Virtually everything that is said negatively can also be said positively. It's the old decision about whether the glass is half full or half empty—it all depends on your perspective. The technique is the same for nearly all negatively phrased questions: Turn the negative to a positive, then follow with the answer and ignore the hostility, the whiny tone, or the guilt dig that usually accompanies these questions.

# CHAPTER 10
## Getting Someone Else to Answer the Question

The person who is asked a question is occasionally not the person best equipped to answer it, especially in group situations. Anytime you are speaking with more than one other person, one of the following three alternatives to redirect the question may be the best way to get the ideal response:

- redirect the question to a colleague if one is present (There are "Absolutely Positively Rules" that govern this redirection; see p. 74.)
- redirect the question to another member of the audience, either a specific person (in which case the same rules apply) or to the general audience
- redirect to the seeker (in certain situations—see below)

Examine the third option first. Many times a difficult question is made so by the vehement demands of the questioner, who actually is looking for a forum or platform for his views. Sometimes it works best just to let him talk, by asking for those views.

## Let Them Speak—Or Not?

Some speakers believe it is never a good idea to give that hostile or difficult person the floor. This thinking suggests that to allow a forum for an opposing idea will cause your own performance to be less than successful. There certainly are instances where that is true. And you do run risks with this approach, especially if you are not sure that you can regain control.

But consider the positive possibilities first. In certain kinds of in-house gatherings, such people will be heard. In meetings of the board, the stockholders, the faculty, or the staff, it is virtually impossible to keep those kinds of people bottled up. And the odds are that you shouldn't leave them bottled up, even if you are the chair or the president and could ignore them if you wanted to exercise your power. Think of it in the same way that "overcoming objections" is thought of in sales organizations. It's better, in most all sales situations, to discover and overcome as many objections as you can. The objections are there, whether you get them out and discuss them—or not. If you do not get them out and handled, they will still come out. The problem is obvious: When you are not there, who knows what kind of wild explanations will be bandied about? Deal with them. And keep control.

The same is true, exactly, with the kinds of questions

that people ask which have angry exclamation points at the end instead of question marks. Those grumbling malcontents will talk to anybody they can; you are far better off in the long run to let them have their little forum. You respond briefly and then move swiftly on to the next question or the next item on your agenda. This course of action gets the problem behind you, instead of out there roaming around, causing discontent to grow.

## Not an In-House Situation?

If the speaking situation is not an in-house one, a judgment must be made each time. Consider who you are, what your relationship is to the group, whether you are ultimately accountable to them, and whether you can be helped more than hurt by giving the hostile individual a brief platform from which to expound.

In situations where you have decided to let that person speak, listen carefully so that you can pull out the one aspect you wish to respond to, the one point you wish to make. Close off the encounter with your strong remarks. Your comment might be, *It is good to have those views expressed; the key concern for all of us is ———*. Or try, *Thank you for expressing your point of view; you and I agree that ———, and that will be our focus this year.* You are using the strategy "speak to one aspect" (chapter 8), or "respond positively to a negative question" (chapter 9). Deliver this brief line strongly, then turn to another part of the audience with, *Next question?*

What if you do not want to give that person the opportunity to speak? Ask him instead to rephrase the comment into a question: *What exactly are you asking me?* or, *Could you please rephrase that into a question?* Once you get a specific question, use one of the many strategies in these chapters. Look directly at the seeker as you begin your response, but do not give him further eye contact. After you have finished your response, turn firmly to the other side of the room with, *Next question?* or the next item on your agenda.

## Redirect the Question

You are a part of a team presentation or a panel. The question, though addressed to you, is in the area of expertise of some other member of the group. Should you redirect the question to that individual? *Yes*, but only if you follow the Absolutely Positively Rules for doing so. Suppose a member of the audience is an expert on the topic and you imagine he is willing, even eager, to respond. Should you redirect the question to him? Yes, but only if you follow the Absolutely Positively Rules.

## The Absolutely Positively Rules

The Absolutely Positively Rules for redirecting questions to other persons (either colleagues or members of the audience) are essentially the Golden Rule for responders: "Do unto others as you would have them do unto you." There are four aspects:

1. Begin by saying the name of the person to whom

you will address the question, loudly and clearly, so that she is alert to what is about to happen.

2. Once you have her attention, repeat the question clearly; chances are she may have been wool-gathering and not heard the question.

3. Buy her some extra time by giving a bit of explanation about why she is the most qualified to respond. Even if she isn't, you will have bought enough extra time for her to respond better than you would have.

4. Identify the seeker, if possible.

Between a client and a stockbroker, it might go something like this:

CLIENT: *Why have commodities margins been going down so much lately?*
STOCKBROKER: *Jane Jones of our Portland office specializes in commodities; she could give a clear picture of why the margins have been decreasing in the last few months. In fact, she made a special study of commodities margins. Jane, could you respond to Mr. Jackson's query about commodities margins?*

Woe unto you if you do not follow all the steps. You can be drummed out of the firm for dropping a question on a person who wasn't aware she was going to be asked for a response or who didn't hear the question.

Someone who secretly wishes to be friendless at work might respond in this manner—Q: *Why have commodities margins been going down so much lately?* R: *Gosh, that's a tough question to answer; we'll ask our specialist. What do you think, Jane?*

Isn't that a bomb? How would you like to have something like that dumped in your lap? Yet, we have all been guilty of dropping such a bomb at times. In a team situation, the strength of one member equals the strength of the entire team, so if Jane looks or sounds foolish, so do you all. And there goes the project you were bidding on.

What about asking someone from the audience to respond? Your judgment is needed here each time. Base your judgment on these criteria:

- Who is the audience? If you are peers or equals, you can pass along a question.
- What is the purpose of the gathering? If its overall purpose is a collective growth in professional knowledge, you can pass it on.
- Who am I in relation to the audience? If you are there as the authority, the guru, it's best not to pass it on. However, if you are first among equals, passing it on is a compliment.

## Points to Remember

Recognize that in some situations, redirecting the question is a gesture of goodwill or a compliment. Examine the gathering, determine your options, and share the spotlight when you can. Delivery counts; you must redirect the question with a confident tone and a strong presence. Otherwise you appear unprepared.

In other situations you are better off to let that individual speak his piece, by redirecting the question to him. Keep control and your image will be strengthened because you indicate you are not threatened by opposing views. Delivery counts here, too. Read the next chapter carefully.

## The "To Do" List

Make a list of situations and places where you speak, regularly or occasionally. Beside each, note whether it is an instance when you can (or should) allow an antagonist to speak his piece. Also make a note of the speaking situations where it would be appropriate for you to redirect a question to someone in the audience.

# CHAPTER 11

## Delivery—The Real Secret to Success

What counts, finally, is often not so much what you say as how you say it. Remember that people ask questions for many reasons other than just to obtain information. They are trying to find out about you. The tremendous amount of information that you communicate about yourself nonverbally is reflected in your delivery. Many people give mediocre responses with superb delivery; they generally fare better than do those with good responses and mediocre delivery skills. Your personal goal, of course, is both.

The overall strategy is to respond from a position of strength and credibility, not from a position of weakness and vulnerability. You demonstrate this confident position with your delivery.

## Tips on Delivery

Strategic pauses, a strong voice, vocal emphasis on key words, voice variety—these four delivery skills augment the direct responses and enhance the indirect ones as well. Practice your tone, your pauses, and your vocal emphasis when you are driving alone in your car.

To begin, pick a simple sentence such as "*He* said he loves my sister." Each time you repeat it, put emphasis on a different word: "He *said* he loves my sister." "He said *he* loves my sister." "He said he *loves* my sister." "He said he loves *my* sister." And, "He said he loves my *sister*."

What happens? The meaning changes each time you emphasize a different word. This is a wonderful tool in vocal emphasis of key words. Now find some other sentences, fact or opinion, to practice changing with only your voice. Learn the power of your voice, and use it.

After a few tries out loud, you will stop feeling foolish. In your car you can be as extreme as you wish, in varying these delivery skills. You should hear improvement almost immediately. Keep practicing.

Basic theory about pauses was discussed in chapter 6. Remember that pauses are one key to thinking before you speak. Pauses are also powerful delivery tools. Use pauses both to emphasize what you have just said and to introduce a strong idea. They are also useful to let the words sink in to the seeker's mind, and to slow your mind down to search for the exact word you want.

## Eye Contact Counts

Effective eye contact is important in all successful communications. In responding to questions it becomes even more important; when responding to difficult questions from a group, it is vital. One person asks the question, but it was probably on the minds of several. So your responsibility is to the group, not just to the seeker. By employing moving eye contact while you repeat the question and respond, you involve the group as well. Look at people other than the seeker as you repeat the question. Give the seeker quick eye contact at the beginning of the actual response, then look at others throughout the response. It is a good practice to return eye contact to the seeker just as you finish. There are two problems with actually accomplishing that, however: timing is difficult, and the seeker sometimes feels encouraged to ask another question while your eyes are on him.

## Responses That Require Superb Delivery

Two other response options exist that depend for their success almost entirely on your delivery:

1. the candidness of admitting you do not know or do not have the information
2. meeting head-on a tough question that you can answer but would prefer not to answer directly

Both of these options require superb delivery if you want to remain on top of the situation and keep everyone's confidence. And both will gain you new respect, from friend and foe alike.

## "I Don't Know, But..."

Often the best response is the candid one: *I don't know.* What too often happens is that people feel they should know, so they try to fake it. They fumble around in an attempt to cover their lack of knowledge, or else they blush, giggle, or get embarrassed. Everybody can tell, so never mind what you "should" know. Most of the time people don't care if *you* know it; they just want the information. Don't try to fake it. Fumbling around puts everything else you have said in jeopardy. Down goes your credibility. The goal here, as with other difficult questions, is to project an overall sense of poise.

For example, if a sales representative is asked the specifications of a certain product, his response may be a firm, positive, *I don't know—but I'll call you later this morning with those figures*. Notice the extra element of a specific commitment to get the information and to get it to the seeker.

Another response might be, *I don't have those figures in my head. Let me check the drawings and get right back to you*. Or consider this response: *I want to give you the precise numbers; let me double-check them and call you this afternoon*. (Use this one only if you do have a rough idea, though, because the seeker is apt to say that the numbers do not have to be precise.)

Try this approach: *That's a new product and I haven't yet committed the numbers to memory. Will you be in your office after lunch? I'll call you with them.* With each approach, say those three little words without any tinge of embarrassment or lack of confidence. Then be absolutely sure that you make a commitment (the more specific the better, generally) to get the information to that person. In a speaker situation, say, *Give me your card after the session so I can get the information to you.*

Even better, though, is just to think the *I don't know, but . . .* and open your mouth to speak when you get to the action you promise to take. Say, *Let me call you about those figures right after this meeting;* or, *I can find out the exact amount with one quick phone call. Stay right here.* This strategy takes practice, but in time you will find it easy to speak with confidence even when you don't know an answer.

## The Direct Approach to a Tough Question

Yes, you should sometimes tackle the tough questions straight on. It is impressive and also refreshing, especially coming from politicians, bureaucrats, and management. The individual who can respond forthrightly gets some additional points for credibility from her audience and even from her antagonists and opponents. Delivery is the total key here; in fact, if you are good enough at delivering these words, you may not need most of the other material in this book. An honest tone and well-timed pauses are essential. Consider this exchange between a political candidate and a taxpayer:

TAXPAYER: *Will taxes go up if we approve this addition to the highway system?*

CANDIDATE: *Taxes* will *go up. [pause] When we compare the 3 percent per thousand increase with the cost of automobile repairs caused by these poorly surfaced roads people will find that their overall cash out of pocket will be less because automobile repairs should go down significantly.*

Notice the emphasis on *will*; notice the pause after the affirmative statement that lets the message sink in. It is important that there is no *but* or *however* to signal what the audience would feel is another *Here she goes again with an excuse*. This is explanation, not an excuse.

Here's an exchange between a CEO and a stockholder:

STOCKHOLDER: *I heard that our dividends will be less this year. Is that true?*
CEO: *It is true. [pause] The economy is still depressed, sales have not yet regained their momentum, and the results are that profits are down across the board.*

The pattern of the words varies with the direct approach. What you see here is the same information as with an indirect approach; the difference is that the answer, the bad news in this case, is right up front. Make sure that you are able to give these direct responses to bad-news questions when you need to. Practice your delivery.

## How Long Should You Respond to Open-Ended Questions?

Delivery tips should include a primer in reading the seeker's nonverbal clues, too. These clues are particularly important when you have been asked an open-ended question to which you are fairly certain that the seeker wants a full response. Three such instances are job interviews, when meeting a superior for the first time, and in an evaluation interview. The question should be an open, *Tell me about yourself*; or *Describe how you felt about that*; or, *Tell me about your experiences with* ———.

Seekers will communicate nonverbally how long you should talk. This message can be demonstrated in two basic positive ways. One such signal is the nodding of the head as you enthusiastically describe your feelings. The other is a soft, murmured expression such as *I see* or *hmmm* or *Okay*. The key is the low volume. You can hear it, but it is not loud enough to be an interference. Both of these messages signal, *Keep talking*.

If the *I see* or *Okay* is delivered at normal, or higher, volume, the seeker is indicating that he has heard enough. You must stop. An interviewer can also nonverbally signal this desire by looking back at your résumé, picking up your evaluation sheet, or turning back to the desk. Stop as soon as you can.

Sometimes, especially in casual conversation, people do not signal; their eyes just glaze over. This message is harder to pick up because we are usually so involved in our own enthusiasm that we do not notice the eyes as quickly as we should. Remember the concept of the contract that two people unconsciously make in order to communicate successfully. For a dialogue to develop, both need to contribute. If you go on at length (even with an open-ended question) you are giving a monologue.

So, thinking on your feet also means not responding at

length every time you are asked an open-end question. I was reminded of this "don't give a speech" aspect from personal experience recently. I had been hobbling around in a wood-bottomed bootie for a month or so. Nearly everyone I saw exclaimed, *What happened?!*

The thinking part here should have involved following my own advice: make it a conversation, not a monologue. It also should have involved deciding whether the seeker really wanted to know all the wonderful details. Most of the time it would have been appropriate for me to say, *Oh, I had a bit of surgery on my toe*, or, *I broke a small bone in the ball of my foot*. The average person would have responded, *Gee, I'm sorry*, or *Hope it's getting well*, and the conversation would have continued to other topics.

But was I smart enough to realize that at first? Not on your life! I was so fascinated by the two events of the foot that I usually launched into the whole story, regardless of who was asking. Only after seeing eyes glaze over less than halfway through the spinning of my glorious story did I finally realize that I was boring people by not thinking before I spoke . . . and spoke . . . and spoke.

Some people did want to know the details. They asked a follow-up question: *Why did you need an operation?* or, *Well, tell me all the details*. And I did. But even then I paused every so often to allow the seeker to get a word in edgewise, so that we had a conversation.

The lesson to be learned here is that even if the seeker is a good friend and even if you have a wonderful story to tell, think on your feet and build a dialogue.

## Points to Remember

What kind of delivery techniques are needed? (1) Absolute confidence projected in your tone; (2) special emphasis on the key words, (3) effective use of pauses for emphasis, (4) special eye contact for your purposes and to read your audience. These techniques are particularly necessary when you respond *I don't know*... and when you answer a tough question directly.

## The "To Do" List

Jot down two or three *I don't know* responses to some specific questions that people ask you. Writing them down will help you remember to use this approach; practicing the responses will help you to respond smoothly and with confidence.

# CHAPTER 12

## Opportunities to Buy Time When Responding over the Telephone

When the seeker who is asking a difficult question cannot see you, a variety of tactics can help you to move the communications along, while keeping you in control. The overall secret once again is the successful delivery of the tactic. Anytime you are asked a question on the telephone to which you would like a few seconds or minutes to frame the most appropriate response, find a way either to call the person back or to get him to hold.

- *I'm in a colleague's office; let me get back to my desk.*
- *I picked up this call in the conference room; can I call you right back?*
- *John, you've caught me in a meeting; are you in your office? I'll get right back to you with those numbers.*

- *My secretary has that folder on his desk; hold just a second and I'll get it. I want to give you the exact numbers, not an estimate.*

You get the idea. The caller does not know what the actual situation is; he simply wants the information. You buy seconds or minutes to look at the numbers, phrase the appropriate response, and pick up the telephone again. Remember to commit to a specific time to get back to him. This strategy works well provided that your tone is confident and poised; you will sound foolish only if your delivery is stumbling or hesitant.

Are you fibbing? Not at all. Your ultimate goals, remember, are effective communication of the required information; good client, or management, or personal relations; and credibility. You achieve these three goals by being in control of your end of the communication and by relaying the information in a manner that best meets the requirements of the relationship.

# CHAPTER 13

# Beyond Questions: Other Opportunities to Think on Your Feet

Other occasions demand that you think on your feet. One such occasion is when discussing a project with colleagues, supporters, or friends. Sometimes you join in, but at other times your mind drifts. Gradually—or suddenly—the conversation shifts to another topic: your topic. Can you take full advantage of this chance to make points?

As you attend meetings, conferences, seminars, and workshops, you are sometimes asked to "say a few words" about a project near to your heart. Sadly, though, it's often less near to your mind. Can you buy enough time to gather your thoughts and make your presence felt?

At those same gatherings you are frequently asked to stand up and introduce yourself. You know how inadequate most people sound:

- *Uh, I'm uh Jack Spratt and uh I own a small print shop. We uh are located on Thirty-fourth Street uh and we'd uh like to have you uh come by.*
- *Let's see. My name is Janice Dogood and I'm a consultant and I consult with people about their colors and about their images and I think images are so important and I'm just glad to be here!*

You've heard them. You have heard people blow their grand opportunity to make an excellent professional or personal impression to a group of people who are important to them. Yet, what they want and need to say are the most basic facts about themselves: their name, where they're from, and what their connection to the meeting is. Not exactly difficult or threatening information, is it?

The same unfortunate response occurs when people are sitting around a luncheon or banquet table. People exchange basically the same information, and most of them do it poorly. The key question at the table is, *What do you do?* As a communications consultant, I am concerned about the numbers of professional people I know who do not have a smooth, professional response to that simple question. Many people give a too short answer: *I'm a lawyer*, or, *I'm a teacher*, or, *I sell insurance.* Here is an opportunity to add the one main piece of support we have discussed, to make an impression and to begin to build the dialogue that is so important. Consider:

- *I'm an attorney. My firm specializes in labor relations.*
- *I'm in the philosophy department at Portland Community College. I teach ethics and morality.*

- *My firm is XYZ Assurance Company; we handle homeowners' and auto insurance clients.*

These introductions are better. And if for some reason you do not like the sound of the exact word that identifies your profession, it is easy to rephrase it in such a way that you do feel good saying it. I have clients who had spent years hating to say that they were "consultants." My solution for them: *I am a partner in a management consulting practice. We specialize in assisting financially troubled companies.* The emphasis is on *partner, management*, and *practice*; the word *consultant* is buried. The second sentence goes on immediately to emphasize a specific area of expertise.

You may hate to say *salesman* or *teacher* or whatever. In such cases, you might begin with the name of your firm and add your role or title second: *I work for Jones and Jones, the environmental engineering firm. I handle the marketing end.*

You can also begin with *My profession is ———*, or, *I'm in the ——— profession.* Whatever you say, say it with pride and confidence. Do avoid the euphemisms that irritate people, such as "sanitation engineer" or "waitperson."

## Representing Yourself with Poise

Is this poor representation of ourselves a problem? I think it is. Is this problem easily solved? Absolutely. It's a problem because you have intentionally put yourself in a situation where you want to make an impression, and then you blow it! We go to conferences and meetings generally because we care about what is going on. The opportunity is ripe for business contacts, marketing, support for ideas, and team-building needs. Whether you are a parent seeking support from other parents for your proposal to develop a teen center in your area, a sales rep with a fine product, or a consultant offering your services, the others at the meeting or at your table are all potential allies, clients, or customers.

The solution? There are several aspects, actually:

- Acknowledge the frustration that you feel when you have not sounded as you wanted to sound.
- Resolve to do something so that next time you will sound more poised.
- Realize that the same three basic items are going to be needed next time, and script out ways to express those facts that please you.
- Practice, practice, practice.

Your goal is to have it roll smoothly, confidently off your tongue at the drop of a luncheon napkin. Jot down possibilities until you find one that pleases you. Then practice saying it in the car after you finish with "He said he loves my sister."

## Saying a Few Words

In other situations where you are asked to "say a few words," do just that. Say a few words. Most people babble on at such length that their opportunity turns into a liability. Follow the same strategies as for responding to questions. Briefly:

- Buy time by standing up slowly or by walking toward the front of the room.
- Pause to organize your thoughts. Find the one key point that you want to express in this situation.
- Don't open with *Thank you, Martha, it's a privilege to be here*. Do not waste that key first sentence with emptiness. State your point while you have their attention.
- State that one main thought firmly and with good pauses for emphasis.
- Add one supporting statement or piece of evidence.
- Repeat your point and stop. (Resist saying "thank you" here, too. The audience will remember your last words; those words should be your point.)

As part of your opener, it is a good idea to repeat what was requested, for exactly the same reasons you repeat the question when you are part of a group (chapter 5):

- buys you time to think
- helps you adjust the request slightly to fit your agenda or purpose
- allows you to present a complete piece of information: the request plus the statement

Once in a while you need to tell bad news. Adopt an indirect approach to soften the blow, perhaps to bury the negative in the middle. Consider this example:

CHAIR OF THE COMMITTEE: *Say, Marian, explain for the group why we lost the BCA account.*
(I'm unprepared for this direct hit, so I rise slowly from my chair, walk toward the chairman, and say):
*Jim, it's very important for us to understand the lessons of the BCA situation. We can improve our approach through what we learned.* [You can see that I'm "buying time" here.] *The BCA wanted a precise plan of action and our team focused on our knowledge of the industry and trends to follow. We'll include some early involvement for the next presentation.*

Not bad for thinking on my feet; however, how foolish of me not to have been prepared. Prepare some thoughts prior to a meeting or other function where you may be asked to say a few words about a project. Make a habit of considering what you might be asked about. Even better, assume you will be asked. Have something to say. You'll amaze and impress others with your "impromptu" skills.

When a client calls me for some urgent help on damage control he is apt to exclaim, *Was I ever caught off guard by that question!* My reaction tends to be, *How could you be surprised by a question about such a hot topic in your industry?*

How can you *not* be prepared to talk about whatever it is you are doing? You run into your supervisor in the coffee lounge. She asks you to give her a quick update on your current task, the Uptown Mall. Adopting another strategy from responding to questions, buy time with a choice question, requiring her to select the aspect she most wants to hear about:

YOU: *The Uptown Mall project is progressing nicely. Do you want to hear first about the politics of the project or about the costs?*
SUPERVISOR: *I'm interested primarily in the politics; overseeing the cost side is John's responsibility now.*

If you had just begun talking you might have picked costs, because they are simpler to describe. She would likely have become impatient because you weren't getting to the point—her point. By forcing her to make a decision, you improve the possibility that your comments will be what she actually wants to know. Use of the word *first* is reassuring to her, indicating that you are equally ready to talk about either aspect.

## Funny One-Liners

What about funny one-liners that you hear people toss off in response to questions? Why haven't those been covered here? Well, they're great if you're Don Rickles. Humor depends for its funniness on poking fun at or ridiculing something or someone. You risk putting down the seeker (or someone else in the audience). Having a laugh at the seeker's expense may seem like good fun at the time. And sometimes it appears to work. But it usually will come back to haunt you. It is true that some people can get away with it. They know the audience, the seeker, the institution being poked fun at. They are masters of timing and excellent judges of good taste. Often you will note that the person they make fun of is themselves. Even then, the joke can backfire. Is there anyone among us who hasn't been offended by a speaker's misplaced humor? Trying to be funny when answering questions is too risky unless you're a professional whose goal is to be funny.

Your goals are more serious:

- effective communication
- good human relationships
- a poised, confident presentation

Resolve to practice the tips in this book so that you can achieve these goals and become a pro at thinking on your feet.

## The "To Do" List

Write out several ways in which you can describe who you are and what you do. Put the emphasis on different aspects of your title, your company's purpose, your duties; see which you like best. You may want to create one for peers and another for clients or customers. Practice them so much that when you go to your next lunch meeting or conference you can express them smoothly.